*The New Novello Choral Edition*

# JOHANN SEBASTIAN BACH

# *Magnificat* in E flat (BWV243a)

for solo voices, SATB chorus and orchestra

Vocal score

Edited, with a new translation of the four Lauds,
by Neil Jenkins

Order No: NOV079026

**NOVELLO PUBLISHING LIMITED**
14 - 15 Berners Street, London W1T 3LJ

It is requested that on all concert notices and programmes acknowledgement is made to 'The New Novello Choral Edition'.
*Es wird gebeten, auf sämtlichen Konzertankündigungen und Programmen 'The New Novello Choral Edition' als Quelle zu erwähnen.*
Il est exigé que toutes notices et programmes de concerts, comportent des remerciements à 'The New Novello Choral Edition'.

Orchestral material is available on hire from the Publisher.
*Orchestermaterial ist beim Verlag erhältlich.*
Les partitions d'orchestre sont en location disponibles chez l'editeur.

Permission to reproduce the Preface of this Edition must be obtained from the Publisher.
*Die Erlaubnis, das Vorwort dieser Ausgabe oder Teile desselben zu reproduzieren, muß beim Verlag eingeholt werden.*
Le droit de reproduction de ce document à partir de la préface doit être obtenu de l'éditeur.

Cover illustration: facsimile of the first page of Bach's autograph score of Magnificat in E♭.
Reproduced by permission of the Staatsbibilothek zu Berlin – Preußischer Kulturbesitz, Musikabteilung mit Mendelssohn-Archiv (Berlin State Library Music Department with Mendelssohn Archive). [Mus.ms.Bach P 38, 1. Notenseite]

© 2008 Novello & Company Limited

Published in Great Britain by Novello Publishing Limited
Head office: 14 - 15 Berners Street, London W1T 3LJ
Tel +44 (0)207 612 7400          Fax +44 (0)207 612 7545

Sales and Hire: Music Sales Distribution Centre
Newmarket Road, Bury St Edmunds, Suffolk, IP33 3YB
Tel +44 (0)1284 702600          Fax +44 (0)1284 768301

Web: www.musicroom.com          www.chesternovello.com

# CONTENTS

# PREFACE

The *Magnificat* in D (BWV243) has long been regarded as one of Bach's finest short choral works and is frequently performed on festive occasions. Far less well known is the work on which it is based, *Magnificat* in E flat (BWV243a), dating from 1723, Bach's first year as Kantor at the Thomaskirche in Leipzig. According to Robert L. Marshall, Bach had the luxury of almost six weeks in which to prepare this work together with a setting of the Sanctus, BWV238, and revisions of Cantata BWV63 for performance on Christmas Day, 1723[1]. Consisting of twelve movements, plus four extra pieces - the Christmas Lauds - the *Magnificat* in E flat is double the length of his normal weekly cantatas, giving Bach the opportunity to impress his new employers and congregation. It contains many more elaborate choruses than were required for the weekly cantatas, and no *secco* recitatives or four-part chorales, which would have been quick and easy to compose.

The structure and tonal scheme shared by both versions of the *Magnificat* are satisfyingly symmetrical and have long been admired by scholars. The choruses are followed by three groups of solo movements in related keys, the last of which is always for an increased number of singers (thus No. 3 is a solo, No. 6 is a duet and No. 10 is a trio). So as to break up an otherwise long sequence of arias, the chorus returns in No. 4 to sing two appropriate words detached from the previous aria: 'omnes generationes' (all generations'). C.S. Terry noted that a similar device had been used in a *Magnificat* in G minor attributed to Albinoni[2]. Bach used this simple idea to craft twenty-seven bars of majestic counterpoint leading to a splendid climax on a dominant minor ninth chord at bar 24. In what was a bold gesture, this chord is left unresolved (though this was not the case in the later revision). No. 10 employs the *tonus peregrinus*, to which the Magnificat was traditionally chanted, as an instrumental counterpoint to the voices: in the first version this is given to a solo trumpet, and in the revision to unison oboes.

In No. 11 ('Sicut locutus est') a reference to 'our forefathers, Abraham and his seed' inspired Bach to look back at the music of his predecessors in Leipzig, such as Johann Kuhnau (1660-1722), and the music of this movement is written in an old-fashioned *a cappella* fugal style that would have been familiar to earlier congregations. The lesser doxology 'Gloria Patri et filio' reaffirms the work in its home key, and at the words 'sicut erat in principio' ('as it was at the beginning') Bach reintroduces the music of the work's opening bars. Although this device was not unknown to composers of the Baroque, its appropriateness at this point would have appealed to Bach. The composition is full of such delightful word painting: 'dispersit' is vigorously scattered; 'exaltavit' and 'deposuit' graphically depict 'rising' and 'falling'; and, in the closing bars of No. 6, the words 'timentibus eum' ('them that fear him') are sung to a plangent repeated note (particularly at bar 31) which suggests intensely controlled nervousness.

**The Four Christmas Lauds**

In Leipzig it was customary during Christmas to introduce four Lauds (hymns in Latin and German) into the Latin text of the Magnificat - a practice which the civic authorities had tried unsuccessfully to stop in 1702[3]. These Lauds had featured in Kuhnau's settings, evident in a set of parts extant in Leipzig[4]. Bach sets the same texts, in the same order as Kuhnau:

A  a setting of Martin Luther's chorale 'Vom Himmel hoch'
B  'Freut euch und jubiliert', an anonymous text derived from Luke ii, 10
C  a text derived from the greater doxology 'Gloria in excelsis Deo'
D  a verse from 'Virga Jesse', a Christmas hymn dating from the late sixteenth century

In Bach's manuscript these pieces are grouped together at the end with indications as to where they should be placed within the work, suggesting that they were not originally planned as part of the work but added as an afterthought. Whether this was as a result of Bach learning at a late stage of composition that he had to follow the precedent set by his predecessors, abandoning an early plan

1    R.L. Marshall: *On the origin of the Magnificat, The Music of Johann Sebastian Bach* (New York: Schirmer, 1989)

2    C.S. Terry: *Bach: The Magnificat, Lutheran Masses and Motets* (London, 1929).

3    M. Geck: 'J.S. Bach's Weinachts-Magnificat und sein Traditionszusammenhang', *Musik und Kirche* xxxi (1961).

4    Musikbibliothek der Stadt Leipzig, Sammlung Becker III.2.124.

to use material already written by Kuhnau, or considering these movements to be optional, we shall not know for certain. But Marshall (op. cit.) describes how, far from being composed in the same style as the rest of *Magnificat*, these interpolations seem to survey a range of previous historical styles of vocal music. 'Vom Himmel hoch' is a cantus firmus motet in the strict *stile antico*. 'Freut euch und jubiliert' is polyphonic, with an independent basso continuo and pairs of voices moving in parallel motion that recalls the motets of Monteverdi, or an earlier setting of the same text (1603) by Sethus Calvisius - himself a Thomaskantor in the early seventeenth century. 'Gloria in excelsis Deo', with its violin obbligato, proceeds in a homophonic fashion reminiscent of Carissimi's later Italian style, as cultivated by the Thomaskantors Johann Schelle, Kuhnau and others. 'Virga Jesse', by contrast, is the most contemporary in style, being written as a florid operatic duet for soprano and bass soloists with continuo. This last Laud introduces the only problem in providing a new performing edition of BWV243a, since the last page of the manuscript is missing, leaving 'Virga Jesse' incomplete at bar 30 (see below).

*Magnificat* in E flat was published by N. Simrock (Bonn) in 1811 as *Magnificat a cinque voci* - with one Laud (C) added at the end - but omitted from the Bachgesellschaft edition (Leipzig, 1851-99). It appeared in the Neue Ausgabe (NBA) in 1955. The four Lauds were published in 1862 in the Bachgesellschaft edition [11. Band, Teil 1] (Laud D incomplete) as an appendix to *Magnificat* in D.

## EDITORIAL PROCEDURE
### Text
The Latin text is the standard version of the Magnificat (taken from Luke i, 46-55) found in the Vulgate bible. Bach's only deviation from this text is his omission of the word 'eius' in the line 'Et misericordia eius a progenie in progenies timentibus eum' (No. 6) rendering its meaning as 'And [his] mercy is on them that fear him'. The fact that C.P.E. Bach and Schütz use the complete sentence in their Magnificat settings seems to indicate that this was an oversight by Bach, rather than a customary change made in Lutheran worship.
### Music
The music of this edition was derived from the *Neuen Bach-Ausgabe* (1955/59). Simrock and Bachgesellschaft edition of BWV243 [11. Band,

Teil 1] were also consulted. Editorial dynamics, instructions and ornaments are shown in square brackets, editorial ties and slurs are shown as 'cut' ties and 'cut' slurs (that is with a stroke through). The editorial continuo realisation is shown in small-sized notes.
### Completition of Laud D
For the completion of the missing portion of 'Virga Jesse', the editor is indebted to Alfred Dürr's preface to his edition of BWV243a in the Bärenreiter Studienpartituren[5]. This reveals that the continuo part to the Duet 'Ehre sei gott in her Höhe' (movement 5 of Cantata 'Unser Mund sei voll Lachens' (BWV110) for soprano and tenor soloists) is very nearly identical to the continuo part of this Laud - albeit in A rather than F. Consequently transposition of this material allows it to be used from bar 36 onwards to provide a suitable, and completely Bachian, ending. Since the last four bars are identical to the opening four bars, that leaves a mere eleven bars where the editor has to reconstruct the vocal lines above it. This construction is based on the phrase lengths and patterns of the vocal lines in corresponding passages of BWV110.
### Dynamics
Bach used dynamics sparingly in BWV243, sometimes using them to indicate the difference between an orchestral ritornello and an accompanying passage. A limited number of editorial dynamics have been added to the present edition.
### Appoggiaturas
Editorial appoggiaturas have been added where they are missing from a passage when repeated.

## THE REHEARSAL PIANO ACCOMPANIMENT
I have provided a new rehearsal accompaniment, in which the material based on instrumental parts is in full-sized type and editorial realisation shown cue-sized. I have tried to represent all of the orchestration, although it has not been possible to preserve every part at the correct pitch.

## THE ORCHESTRAL SCORE AND PARTS
The score and parts, available on hire from the publisher, are newly engraved and correspond exactly with this vocal score. The orchestral parts may be used for either period or modern

---

5    A. Dürr: Preface to *J.S. Bach: Magnificat*, Bärenreiter *Studienpartitur 58*, (Kassel, 1959), pp.iv, vi.

instrument performances. A newly-realised Keyboard Continuo part is suitable for chamber organ or harpsichord.

The orchestration of the *Magnificat* in D is 2 flutes, 2 oboes, 3 trumpets, timpani and strings.

**Oboes** Bach's requirements were for two players doubling oboe and oboe d'amore. Transpositions of the d'amore music (Nos. 3 & 4) are given in an appendix to the part, this allowing the whole piece to be played on two oboes.

**Trumpets and Timpani** Three virtuoso players are required, with Trumpet 1 needing to reach d'''. The timpani are tuned to D and A.

**Strings** The string parts contain all the bowing and articulation found in the MS.

**Keyboard Continuo**
This is the part from which the continuo should be played. The vocal score is no adequate substitute since it is a piano reduction for rehearsal purposes. The keyboard continuo part contains the few continuo figures found in the MS.

ACKNOWLEDGEMENTS
Thanks are due to Hywel Davies for his help in seeing this edition through to publication.

*Neil Jenkins*

NOTE
The Novello edition of *Magnificat* in D was published in 1874 with an English translation by the Reverend John Troutbeck (1832-99), loosely based on the text found in The Book of Common Prayer. In the present edition the only English translations provided are those for the Christmas Lauds.

# MAGNIFICAT in E flat

**1** **[CHORUS]**

[Tpts., Timp., Obs., Stgs., Cont. Org.]

## 2 [ARIA]

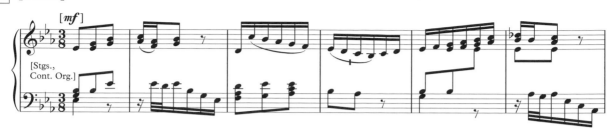

[mf]

[Stgs.,
Cont. Org.]

SOPRANO 2 SOLO

Et ex-sul - ta - vit spi - ri - tus_ me - us,

[p]

[mf]

et ex-sul - ta - vit spi - ri - tus_ me - us,

[p]

14

**[A. 1st Christmas Laud]**

Chorus

19

**4** **[CHORUS]**

* no accidentals are given in the MS: this phrase corresponds with the same passage in the D major setting

**5** **[ARIA]**

BASS SOLO

Qui-a fe-cit__ mi-hi mag-na,

**[B. 2nd Christmas Laud]**

6 [DUET]

ALTO SOLO [p]

Et mi - se - ri - cor - di - a,_____ mi - se - ri - cor - di - a_____ a pro - ge -

TENOR SOLO [p]

Et mi - se - ri - cor - di - a,_____ mi - se - ri - cor - di - a_____ a pro - ge - ni - e

- ni - e in_____ pro - ge - ni - es;

in_ pro - ge - ni - es, in_ pro - ge - ni - es;

**7** **[CHORUS]**

* In the D major version this note is the same as the note for the Basses, although no accidental is given in the E♭ version

* In the D major version this note is the same as the note for the Basses, although no accidental is given in the E♭ version

* In the D major version this note is the same as the note for the orchestral Bass, although no accidental is given in the E♭ version

* This note is given as A♮ in Urtext, and therefore breaks the pattern set in bars, 1,5,9 and 13. In the D major version, however, it still agrees with the bass note.

**[C. 3rd Christmas Laud]**

**Chorus**

8 [ARIA]

TENOR SOLO

De - po - - - su - it, de-

et ex - al - ta - - - - - vit hu - mi - les.

9 [ARIA]

**[D. 4th Christmas Laud]**

[Cont. Org.]

SOPRANO SOLO

Vir - ga Jes - se flo - - - - - -
*Jes - se's stem is flo - - - - - -*

BASS SOLO

Vir - ga Jes - se flo - - - - -
*Jes - se's stem is flo - - - - -*

In - du - it car - nem ho - mi - nis, fit
*Hu - man form, so meek and mild, is*

In - du - it car - nem ho - mi - nis, fit pu - er de - lec -
*Hu - man form, so meek and mild, is ta - ken by this*

pu - er de - lec - ta - - - - - - - - - - - -
*ta - ken by this ho - - - - - - - - - - - -*

-ta - - - - - - - - - - - - -
*ho - - - - - - - - - - - - -*

* Editorial reconstruction from here to end of movement (see Preface)

## 10 [TRIO]

## 11 [CHORUS]

**12** **[CHORUS]**

Chorus